INDUSTRIAL RELATIONS IN MODERN INDIA

Concepts and Ideas

Srikanth Goparaju

To close friends, family members, and relatives who have given me the confidence to write about Equal Remuneration provisions (Now included in the Code on Wages Act, 2019), and other Industrial Acts – difficult topics to write about in this part of the world.

Simply complying with equal remuneration principles can transform India.

SRIKANTH GOPARAJU

LIABILITIES AND DISCLAIMER

No Liability

The author and/or the publisher is not liable for any loss or damage caused to any person or institution who may act or take decisions based on the information presented in this book. No claim is made regarding accuracy, completeness, or correctness of information presented here.

Changes due to amendments or changes in the law

Periodic improvements and changes in the law have now become common. Although, every effort is made to bring the most recent developments to the reader; it is possible that the laws, rules, and regulations have changed. Also, new errors may have emerged that cannot be detected yet given we are dealing with new provisions or new laws. The reader must accept these possibilities.

Also, earlier versions of the book may have taken information Bills submitted in Lok Sabha in 2019 for the relevant Acts which were cleared by Parliament of India in September 2020. Some of the accepted recommendations of the Standing Committee dealing with Labour Reforms that show in the Acts of 2020 may be different. This was a source of minor potential errors. This book is updated up to March 2021.

Errors

The author reserves all rights to amend or correct arithmetic, grammatical, or spelling errors at any time. Further, the author can make improvements in the content of the text at any time without providing any notice of the same to any party.

Names of individuals and places or events

Names of individuals and places or events within the book were created to illustrate concepts and are not representative of any person, organization, or event as such.

Names of companies

Names of companies in cases have been used as per current professional practice in business and academic literature.

Suitability of the book

The book is suitable for study for all ages and for international readers. It is intended that the management student and professional in India may find it useful.

FOREWORD

This book is written for management professionals and students who are interested in labour law, industrial relations, and allied subjects related to the welfare of employees and workers.

The book can be used as part of an MBA or PGDM program as a reference text for industrial relations and labour law subjects.

The very nature of the subject is dynamic, and changes may be initiated by worker organizations, the government at various levels, or the businesses. While there may be some agreement on material facts, there is likely to be divergence of perspectives on how best to address industrial relations issues.

Srikanth Goparaju

INTRODUCTION

Writing a book must be easy for a scholar. However, a subject such as 'Industrial Relations' can be a demanding one, especially in a society that is undergoing change.

There are divergent perspectives and views – especially those of the workers. Often the issues and problems facing a certain stakeholder group may not find adequate representation in the popular publications of the day such as newspapers and magazines, and popular shows and talks on electronic media.

While big business, billionaires, and tech wizards have captivated the attention of the world in recent times; the poor worker, the labourer, and the junior office staff continue to contribute and persist in their own small way all over the world. So, while 'industrial relations' may not be a 'happening topic' for the layperson; from an academic and managerial standpoint it has grown in importance.

The focus of the book is on the learner and the student of the subject. Industrial Relations is a specialized branch and one would expect future managers, leaders, and aspiring professionals to take a keen interest in it.

It was a personal struggle to write within this domain. Many ideas and versions of the text were rejected. This was because those versions did not meet the standards set by the author for what would really benefit the student and professional.

This project was taken up in 2017-18 while the author was seeking out suitable academic opportunities. He tried to make it fun to work on this project despite the personal struggle involved.

SCOPE OF THE BOOK

This text takes a different approach to the subject of industrial relations. It is hard to categorize or group it into a certain type of writing. A list of different ways in which one can study the topic and the approach taken in this book is presented below.

The subject of industrial relations can be studied from a historical standpoint as is normally done in most studies in different parts of the world. Here various events and government initiatives are historically described. The gradual evolution of the field and the emergence of organizations such as trade unions is studied and described.

Governments often come up with legislative initiatives such as introducing a Bill and attempting to pass it. There are objects and reasons for any legislative intervention. A study of these initiatives by the Government can be another approach to industrial relations.

Scholars normally do a review of academic literature developed over the years. These may comprise concepts and theoretical frameworks proposed by various social scientists. A review of these works is often a starting point for the study of any subject.

A fourth approach could examine the various institutions that are operating in the field of labour welfare and human resources. A study of these institutions and their positions can help us understand the dynamics better. Indeed, this would provide a cross sectional view of what is happening in the field.

In contrast to the methods mentioned above, this book looks at the practical dimensions examining the field from that of a learner and a practitioner who seeks to operate, influence, and manage challenges. The emphasis is on Indian labour laws. Various terms are used based on their legislative connotations rather than what is understood by the layman.

PLANS FOR SUBSEQUENT EDITIONS

Every author wants to write a book that is perfect and complete. However, there are competing pressures. On the one hand, the book must be brought out quickly for the benefit of the readers who value the content and would gain from reading it. On the other hand, the author's desire to make the product better and better exists.

No matter however great the result, the creator knows that more is possible. However, it is not clear if after all that the author wants were to be incorporated in the book; it would indeed become a great product. It is really a question of which path one must take in writing. The path toward further refinement would make a technically robust product but with too much detail and excessive precision to a fault. The same effort toward precision could be better expended in explaining and elaborating on important aspects of the subject. So, one must choose between making a point well and making enough good points that educates the reader about industrial laws.

Nevertheless, what could the other *path* be? This is something that can be explored in a subsequent edition, if at all necessary. What could that edition contain?

Greater *precision* could be brought into the numbers used in the text such as those of the wage ceilings. For example, a certain enactment may have INR 24,000 p.m. as a wage ceiling. Is it equal to and more than or merely more than the ceiling? These finer points will certainly be encountered by the practitioner, although an author or writer may skip this item of detail.

Second, how far must one go with the *State specific* amendments? There are Central Rules and regulations of corporations and Scheme details. Should one be comfortable with the broad import of the provisions or should one concern with the minute details? Another edition could have ventured into using these details weaving them into lucid explanations.

What about *case laws*? Haven't important questions in labour law been settled through the precedence of the case? But should we burden the student with these matters early on? If we examine the issue of Equal Remuneration, we can see that compliance itself of the relevant provisions of the law is so poor. What purpose is served in engaging in legal tangles and debates early on in one's education? Should the learner focus instead on *compliance* with commonly accepted legal principles?

This takes us to another point of how the different welfare schemes have fared. An assessment of this can be very valuable. For example, one could examine how many members are now beneficiaries of Provident Funds or what percentage of establishments are now covered. One can even ask how these numbers have grown over time. Would it not be interesting to know if a certain advisory board has been set up in Mizoram as per provisions of a welfare Act? Another edition could possibly focus on these dynamic numbers.

Such nuanced aspects can be covered in another book suitably titled '*Advanced Industrial Relations*' or in additional volumes to this book, if necessary. All said and done, this edition is extremely useful and valuable as it is.

PART I: GETTING TO WORK

CHAPTER 1

Industrial Relations around you

"India is one of the richest nations on earth, some residents the most opulent of them all, but more importantly India is a labour wealthy nation and her people are the finest."

Rajesh and Shwetha are siblings who live in Shyampur and go to study at B.K. College. Rajesh is studying in a management program and is currently attending classes for a subject called 'Industrial Relations'.

On the way back from school, Shwetha looks at the book "Industrial Relations in Modern India" written by one Srikanth Goparaju.

Shwetha asks Rajesh about the course - "What is industrial relations[i]?" Rajesh goes on to explain in his own words, "Industrial relations is about workers and organizations and their interrelationships. It is about the two parties achieving their goals together. Some negotiation is needed to settle differences, though."

Shwetha says, "Okay, it sounds more like joint discussion between the two parties – I heard the term 'collective bargaining'. Is that all there is to it? Can you think of some situations where this subject may be relevant?"

Rajesh realizes that he has not thought through the term. One must be very clear about what different terms mean and any type of vagueness or ambiguity in definitions could be misinterpreted. He thinks back at the various situations that they routinely face.

Situation 1: Transportation

It is Thursday morning Rajesh and Shwetha are preparing for their class. Rajesh takes the local RTC bus. The conductor smiles at him. Rajesh is curious how the employees in the State Transporter are organized?

Situation 2: Banks

Shwetha wants to visit the bank to create a demand draft for an application. However, the bank employees are on strike. So, she can't get the work done. She wonders why the bank workers are agitating.

She visits a web site related to the Bank employees' association[ii] to learn more.

Situation 3: Information Technology

Rajesh speaks to his cousin who is working in the Information Technology field. He informs him that he is studying and preparing for 'Industrial Relations' classes. He is curious how employees are organized in the software industry. There are not many trade unions for software employees. How are their grievances addressed?

Rajesh goes on to explain, "So industrial relations is an important subject that consists of three generic groups of players: the employer, the worker or the employee, and the government. There could be other players too, but I am thinking in a simplistic manner." Rajesh goes on to elaborate on the role of the government from what he learnt in the book.

Government

Shwetha asks, "What can governments do to help workers or businesses?"

Rajesh says, "A lot. The role of Government has changed over the last few decades in India in its dealings with businesses. Governments can foster prosperity and well-being."

Shwetha, "How so?"

Laws

Rajesh says, "Okay, let's first understand what is meant by law.

In our country law is made by the legislature, implemented by the executive, and interpreted by the judiciary. There may be some overlap of these functions in different circumstances. Such overlaps have been witnessed throughout history and in the constitutional arrangements seen in different parts of the world.

In India, laws or Statutes are created or made by the Parliament and State Legislatures. A local body too has certain powers on specific subjects. These usually apply within the local areas. This heritage of the Panchayats (and Municipalities) is recognized in the Constitution as well.

In industrial relations, the term 'appropriate Government' is often used and it is a reference to the Central or the State Government."

An Ordinance is a temporary instrument promulgated by the President – an Act of the Parliament is expected to then replace it at an early date.

Shwetha, "Yeah. I know that we have a federal structure. Now with powers delegated to Panchayats and Municipalities this is a three-tiered structure (Some would say 5 tiered, given Zilla and Mandal parishads)[iii]. I learnt all this in High School while you were busy studying Physics and Chemistry."

Rajesh, "True. There is also subordinate legislation[iv] consisting of Rules and Regulations and these must be presented before the Parliament or State Houses (Legislature and Councils where they exist) to retain their validity. Notifications are issued by the appropriate Government say, for example, to extend a Welfare Statute to an industry or a region within India. A provision within the Welfare Statute may allow for such notifications to be issued from time to time."

Shwetha, "I didn't get the last part."

Rajesh, "I meant to say that the Act will contain certain provisions. These provisions will describe when and how the Central Government can issue notifications appointing someone, or extending the Act to some occupation, or extending the Act to a new region or State.

In other words, the law makers expect certain situations to emerge. These situations may require the government to inform affected parties of its actions so that the purposes of the Act are not undermined due to changed circumstances. A provision for notifications allows the Government to clarify its actions, inform affected parties, and extend the Act etc."

Shwetha, "I know all this. Let's come back to the question of how Governments can foster prosperity and wellbeing. What do you think?"

Rajesh, "Legal reformers and the law commission[v] may review and examine the operation and performance of various laws. This may be periodically compared with governance objectives to assess progress. I want to explain three aspects of law – implementation, economic impact, and need for governance. I will take each of these aspects and explain it using 2x2 matrices. My focus would be on labour welfare and management of organizations. Please read the following sections A, B, C."

A. Implementation Matrix

Not all laws are implemented with equal gusto. We frequently find governments interfering in the affairs of individuals, families, or corporations which may or may not be approved in different parts of the world. In many areas of social and economic life, we find Governments stepping in needlessly. Examples may be given here of how Western technology companies are forced to share personal data of users with communist regimes while doing business in those countries. Reports of Government surveillance of private citizens in the West have eroded the concept of 'individual rights' as cherished by liberal democracies.

Reports of sloppy disaster relief efforts from around the world indicate something unusual. We find that governments are less effective than what the public expects of them. Somehow, the mighty power of the State disappears and what is glaring is inefficiency or incompetence in fulfilling its core obligations towards its own citizens.

These situations compel us to think about what the ideal role of should be the Government? While there is no easy and permanent answer, a better way of discussing this can be found.

If we dwell on it a little deeper, we see that having laws and implementing them are two different things. The following matrix shows the different possibilities in a 2x2 format of laws and their implementation. The terms 'feel good legislation' or 'well-meaning legislation' may sound cynical or skeptical but they convey the difference between the categories of law in an easily understandable manner. They may not apply to each enactment rigidly though.

Table 1.1: Implementation Matrix.

Implementation is weak	Strongly implemented

Laws are well defined	Laws are well defined
FEEL GOOD LEGISLATION Feel good legislation under-taken to meet international obligations and welfare commitments to education and health	ACTIVE LEGISLATION These have security and economic impact such as internal or national security laws, employment, finance
Implementation is weak Laws may be non-existent or weak WELL MEANING LEGISLATION Laws meant to encourage good behaviors in citizens and organizations but weakly implemented. Monitoring of citizens or businesses may be delegated to the States, or managed through subordinate legislation, orders or through discretionary powers given to officials involved	Strongly implemented Laws may be non-existent or weak GOVT OVERREACH State interventions to address non-routine disasters, emergency response etc. Can work in a negative manner through covert action against strikers, surveillance of trade union leaders etc.

This matrix may be used as a diagnostic tool to compare the objectives of the government in a certain domain – say labour welfare and the existing state of affairs.

The existing state of affairs has two aspects: First, the spectrum of requirements and expectations of labour and business. The existing body of laws and subordinate legislation must in theory address this range of expectations. Second, the resources and energy committed to the implementation of the body of laws may vary in degree from one Act to another. With time the results and progress achieved may differ too. So, there could be unmet needs and inadequacy in meeting identified needs.

The gaps between the stated objectives and the current situation can suggest future directions for law making or implementation.

B. Arenas of lawmaking

If we assume that one of Government's many roles is to regulate and control the activities of individuals and organizations; the question arises as to what should be an optimal role of government and how it should encourage social and economic development? It is often contended that if there is no regulation, this can encourage undesirable social and economic practices that are eventually harmful to society and business. If there is over-regulation, this can dampen the spirit of enterprise and social interactions.

Most political or business commentators think in terms of over-regulation and under-regulation. Instead, as is common in management theory, a 2x2 matrix can help understand this aspect better. It is helpful to think in terms of two dimensions-more regulation versus less regulation on one hand. Social and economic activities – the target behaviors – whether they are high or low on the other.

This leads to four different arenas of law making and its impact on the economy.

'Playground' is the area where social energies are on an upswing and socio-economic activities are undertaken according to rules that are followed carefully. Winning is important too. The main economic playgrounds are the mainstream activities of any country such as agriculture and irrigation, manufacturing endeavors that create capital goods, tools, and machines that improve productivity and those that are consumed and the service sector including the essential services. The laws made by governments influence the working of companies in this space thereby enhancing prosperity and wellbeing for all.

'Trivia' is the area where economic activities are low, and the role of government is limited too. These include activities such as puzzles, trivial pursuits in arts, games, quizzes, contests, etc. Most of the workforce is not primarily engaged in these pursuits and a preoccupation with them doesn't bring any financial rewards or prosperity as such to society. Normally, Governments keep away from involving, regulating, or controlling such pursuits in a substantial manner.

'Party' is the area where social energies are at play; however, there is no oversight or supervision of actions. In other words, it is party time when social activities are high, but Government involvement is low. Here the social (and economic) energies are set free. Opportunities are often created as a result of technological or demographic changes. For example, platforms may be created for application developers in the field of Virtual Reality. The laws may not be fully defined yet in this new field. This becomes a 'party' arena for small businesses engaged in these projects. Similarly, the discovery of a new market may allow sales to grow giving advantages to early birds. In due course of time, as competition grows, some regulatory controls may be brought in.

'Museum' is where too many laws exist, but they have no relationship to social and economic realities of the day. These laws may have emerged from a set of legacy or outdated practices from a bygone era. Similarly, there are other laws emerging from social and economic practices that evolved out of convenience. Continuing with these laws may serve as a hindrance to growth and development. Business observers know of several areas where often a fortress is created in an industrial field by the government while no enterprise is keen on investing in that particular area. In effect, we may have laws that discuss matters in depth on a dead subject - leading to no real economic value or social benefit.

With these two dimensions we will be able to come up with a 2x2 matrix of Government involvement:

Table 1.2: Arenas of lawmaking.

High economic activity Low Govt Involvement PARTY	High economic activity High Govt Involvement PLAYGROUND
Low economic activity Low Govt Involvement TRIVIA	Low economic activity High Govt Involvement MUSEUM

Government can monitor these arenas for law making and examine its degree of involvement. This serves as a diagnostic tool to assess how laws are impacting social and economic spheres. A cross country comparison (or across States comparison within India) can provide a perspective on choices that can be made here. Some countries may embrace innovation and therefore, have liberal laws for high technology fields. Other countries may be overregulated in certain industries in a dysfunctional manner.

C. Engagement Strategy Matrix

The previous matrix shows how the laws and regulations correspond with the social and economic conditions prevalent at a time and the impact on those conditions. It also shows how legislation can be grouped based on how it affects growth.

The question is how can governments become more relevant?

We can examine two dimensions - where Government should be involved and where Government is engaged. How these choices are made can impact the functioning of individuals and organizations and society at large. A dysfunctional role can be played when government policies are mismatched with societal aspirations leading to litigation, protests, and unrests.

Four roles are explained below. Although phrased in a skeptical tone 'absconder' role is played when various sections of the populace feel neglected or left out. A student looking for scholarships finds very little help from his countrymen and fellow citizens. A poor person who falls ill has to wage a lone battle against her ailments.

In other areas where need for governance is high, we notice that governments are indeed active such as corporate taxes and employment law. The government is reckoned as a player.

Obstructer role is felt when growth of businesses is hampered by regulations that have a delaying effect. They make the entire economic system that much more inefficient. The checks and balances are poorly designed leading to sub optimal system performance.

In certain other areas such as personal financial decisions, operational aspects of small and micro enterprises, we see almost no need for government interference. Usually, governments too do not partake in such activities that may be considered of minor value and having limited national or international impact. Local governments or panchayats may be involved slightly with individuals and businesses.

Table 1.3: Engagement strategy matrix.

Need of governance is high Low Govt Involvement ABSCONDER Welfare, Women's issues, Care of children and elderly, civil liberties, education, primary healthcare	Need of governance is high High Govt Involvement PLAYER Corporate taxes, Securities, Banking, Large corporate financial dealings
Need of governance is low Low Govt Involvement BYSTANDER	Need of governance is low High Govt Involvement OBSTRUCTER/ INTRUDER

Family and social affairs, personal lives, religious choices, operational aspects of micro and small businesses	Economic areas where complicated laws exist or long and arduous procedures that are uneconomical persist

Strategic Choices

Rajesh sums up the discussion, "So, one way in which governments can become more effective is to make appropriate strategic choices of when and how deeply they would engage with individuals, institutions, and corporations. It can begin by recognizing the area or domain that it is operating in, the type of role that it is playing in that situation and choose an appropriate strategy to engage or disengage with those areas.

Governments may choose to play a more active role in which they are reckoned as a key player through additional sophisticated or highly efficient actions thereby strengthening their position. Where governance is needed but not up to the mark, Governments can come up with new initiatives to fulfil their obligations.

Simplifying procedures that are inefficient and being more citizen and market friendly could be strategies used to step back from areas where engagement is dysfunctional.

Similarly, identifying areas where less government would work, governments may choose to use a 'wait and watch' approach or take a more dormant role.

By carefully calibrating its engagement with society, government can be more effective."

Shwetha, "Okay. That is an interesting thought. But why did you not just tell me that Governments have to calibrate their interactions with businesses instead of putting me through all those matrices?"

Rajesh, "I could have possibly done that, but you wouldn't have the tools to analyze and recommend suitable steps."

Chapter Notes

1. The term 'Industrial Relations' is not defined in any of the major labour laws.

2. All India Bank Employees' Association's website is provided.

3. The Constitution was amended, and new articles were added related to urban local bodies and Panchayats.

4. There is no formal definition as such for the term 'subordinate legislation'. This may include Rules, notifications, regulations and so on which must be read together with the main Act.

5. The reform of the Indian legal system is complicated and often recommendations are made on various aspects by the Law Commissions. The Government may initiate lawmaking, repeal outdated laws or provisions thereof, or take other actions based on these recommendations.

Recent Developments – A real life scenario

A trade dispute need not be between an employee and an employer. It can also be between employers and employers. The Confederation of All India Traders has recently taken issue with MNCs entering Indian retail and the potential loss of jobs in the unorganized retail sector. Such confederations may not necessarily be registered under the Trade Unions provisions of Industrial Relations Code, 2020.

These organizations may be registered under the Societies Registration Act, 1860; The Co-operative Societies Act, 1912; or even The Companies Act, 1956. Registration of Trade Unions is void under those other Acts as per the relevant provision. However, the key here is not the legal status of the entity and under which Act it was registered. Rather, the issues it takes up could be investigated. Such disputes would be considered trade disputes (more precisely 'industrial disputes') as per the Industrial Relations Code, 2020, as the concerned matters impact the employment or non-employment of workers. In any case, IR managers should be interested and alert to these developments.

Sources: Derived after reading several articles published in the Times of India, Deccan Chronicle, and The Hindu during 2017-18.

CHAPTER 2

Finding a job

"Work is needed not for serving others but for mastering oneself."

Vinita and Sarla are two sisters living in the North East. Vinita is going to college and Sarla to school.

Sarla asks her elder sister, "Sis, what after college? You are now studying Industrial Relations – is that helpful to you in getting a job?"

Vinita, "Possibly yes. Most of the laws are now consolidated into four codes related to wages, social security, industrial relations, and working conditions. In addition, there are laws related to notification of vacancies and for apprentices that may be immediately helpful to me. Also, these laws require non-discrimination of women in employment matters, so knowing that might help. I can't say specifically how, though."

Vinita adds, "I may have to look for work - Finding work may involve the following activities: communicating with potential employers, going through recruitment and selection processes, and participating in networking events."

The role of the public sector

Vinita enjoys watching sports on television. The other day she saw the women's cricket match between India and Sri Lanka that India won. She likes to cheer for the Indian team. Why? She likes to cheer because she likes her country. She always wanted to do something for India. Maybe she could work for an Indian company and make it successful? This thought came to her mind several times, but she was not sure.

Information about companies was not as easily available as that of the cricket match. She could have tuned in to the business channels. But the focus is mainly on shares and financial performance. There is an occasional interview with the CEO. How is it to work for the company? What are the managers like? This is something she wondered about.

She is aware of the Government at Central and State levels but in India we also have companies/establishments that are called public sector enterprises- What about the public sector? There are good ones – the Maharatna, Navaratna and the like[vi]. She doesn't know much about them except for the occasional advertisement in the papers wherein politicians inaugurate a plant or start a project. Public sector organizations exist both in the Central and State sphere.

How can she find more information about the public sector? She wonders if she could go for a walk-in or do an internship at a nearby enterprise. Visiting the web sites of these companies and reading reports may provide further details.

Generally, public sector jobs are based on public examinations. After engineering studies, students are required to appear for GATE to qualify for engineering positions with public sector organizations. More recently UGC-NET examination is being used to select managerial staff.

Jobs in the private sector too have increased in recent years[vii].

Sarla says, "Would you visit the local employment exchange?"

Career Centers– are they obsolete?

Vinita, "Yes, that's an interesting question you bring up. I always wondered about the exchanges. Now people speak only in terms of stock exchanges!"

Vinita continues, "Here is what I know. Employment exchanges were set up several decades ago. They were created before the information revolution. Job seekers list themselves at these exchanges and they are paired with companies. Ideally, this is how the system is supposed to work. Building a simple computer-based system to achieve this must be easy for India's scientists and technologists. However, we can see that it doesn't work in practice. This highlights the deep differences between what is technologically possible and right and what happens in the real world.

The situation in India is that millions are registered at the exchange, but few have found employment through these exchanges. Practically no professional knows that they do exist. Also, it is unclear if any manager or professional would be inclined to approach them. Despite this, a few crores are already registered with the exchanges. In other words, if every job seeker were to register, this number would be of a higher order.

For lateral entry jobs - Some initiatives have been taken by the government to simplify employment for the public sector at senior levels. The public enterprises selection board (PESB) can help in placing professionals for senior levels such as MD, Director and so on."

Table 2.1 - Facts and Figures in 2018 about job seekers.

- There were 978 exchanges in India in 2018 which include over 14 professional and executive employment exchanges. In 2014, 4.8 crore job seekers were in the live register while 3.93 lakh were placed [1].

> • A new portal called NCS – National Career Service is being further developed. With 3.7 crore job seekers and over 14 lakh employers in late 2016, the database is now growing [1].
>
> • In 2014 the Live Register had about 4.8 crore and above job seekers while only 3.3 lakh got placed. Why are the numbers so disproportionate? If we examine this closely, we see that the vacancies notified ranged from 3.5 to 8.2 lakh only during 2006 to 2014. This is as per Ministry of Labour and Employment Annual Report of 2017 figures.

Sarla says, "Everyone is using computers these days, so why don't you list your profile on a job board?"

Online search engines and job boards

Vinita, "Online job boards claim large number of vacancies but lack of transparency of subsequent processes makes them not particularly useful. For example, we don't know what happens when you apply through them for a job.

Now some information is being shared about the number of applicants for a job. However, we don't know what would happen next. From the public view, it is as if all the resumes go into a black box and nothing further is known.

The core issue can be understood by studying the data from Government annual reports. The demand for jobs is very high, and only a few are being placed. So, this seems to be the problem. Both public sector and private sector are not able to generate enough number of vacancies to meet the demand [viii].

It is a different story that plenty of work needs to be done for the country to move forward. However, this latent need of the country (of plenty of work to be done) is not being converted into manpower plans for different establishments. These manpower plans would then include new positions or vacancies so that the establishment can achieve its goals. Now the question is, even if we make this process more efficient for every establishment would that meet the job demand[ix]?

With creative and innovative plans by state governments and enterprises, feelings of passivity and helplessness, wherever they exist, can be overcome. The Union Ministry is embarking on self-employment as a partial solution. A fuller discussion and more research is needed on employment generation to address this problem. No one in the world seems to know how to solve this. Employment and job seeker matching can always be made easily once enough vacancies are created."

Where to Apply?

Sarla "So you know where you will send your resume?"

Vinita, "Well I don't. I do know the names of a few companies where I could work. Many companies are listing jobs on their web site. However, we need to constantly track the opportunities across many businesses. But the bigger task is choosing the right company. This requires extensive research on the businesses and understanding their individual needs and requirements. Business look up services based on location and other criteria can be made readily available, however, such services are not available freely."

Legal Aspects related to vacancies

India has a law dealing with Employment Exchanges or what are now called Career Centers. It should be regarded as one of the most important legislations in India especially given that we have many job seekers. The provisions related to this are in the Code on Social Security, 2020. However, managers and management education have not given it the priority it deserves.

Table 2.2 - Legal Aspects related to vacancies.

Employment Exchanges are now covered under the chapter related to 'Employment Information and Monitoring'. This chapter is part of Code on Social Security, 2020. The organizations that would handle this aspect are now called Career centers.

- It applies to establishments both in public and private sector and to all vacancies barring a few exceptions. For example, vacancies of employment of less than 90 days or those that would be filled by promotion are excluded.

- Employers are required to notify vacancies to career centers before filling them. Information returns must be submitted to the career centers periodically.

- The Act allows for inspection of returns or records to be carried out, fines to be levied for non-compliance and specific rules are prescribed under the Act.

- The Act applies to all types of vacancies including professional, technical, managerial, and leadership positions.

A proper implementation of the law related to exchanges or what are now called career centers can help track core Government obligation of providing equal opportunity, tackling unemployment, and improving labour mobility.

Also, more can be done to strengthen employment news publications, television and radio programs, and online or offline forums for citizens to discuss job and career opportunities."

Employee

Back in Shyampur, Amul, a friend of Rajesh, is walking by. He waves at them, "Hello. You guys seem to be involved in some argument."

Rajesh, "I am talking about the course I am currently doing. So, what are you up to?"

Amul, "I am working on an assignment on the Indian worker. Apparently, managers in India criticize workers for being low on attendance and motivation. Indian law allows both men and women to work."

Rajesh, "Yes, we are discussing about the IR course too."

Table 2.3 - Facts and Figures in 2018 of Indian worker.

- India has a greater number of young people who are in the working age – if we assume 18 to 60 (in some organizations this may be 62 or even 65) as the working age.

- Agriculture and related fields have the bulk of Indian workers of about 24.6 crore[x]. Manufacturing that includes both public sector and private is another area of the economy

- Finally, service especially by private firms has emerged as the next major sector of Indian economy. Out of a total workforce of 46.5 crore, 2.8 crore are in the organized sector.

Rajesh continues, "The second actor in the industrial relations sphere is the employee. Employee is usually connected with a job. A clear understanding of who a 'worker' or 'employee' is may be needed. Both the terms are used in legislation with their definitions. I feel that we can group workers based on certain criteria. The workers can be grouped by their vulnerability type. Another way is to examine the type of engagement they have with the enterprise. A third category could be the nature of work they perform"

So, a key distinction is whether a worker is in the organized or in the unorganized sector.

Organized sector – These are usually registered firms and the employment is monitored by government agencies.

Unorganized sector – These organizations are outside the purview of government bodies. This sector may include informal labourers such as those employed in farms, unregistered rural or suburban units that are very small to be covered by any legislation.

Table 2.4 - Legal Aspects related to Indian worker or employee.

•   Factories Act, 1948 (Now part of The Occupational Safety, Health and Working Conditions Code, 2020), has a threshold of 20 members without the use of power for example. Many units may be below the threshold to be covered by this law.
A new law for securing social security for unorganized workers (such as domestic help or self-employed) called Unorganized Workers Social Security Act, 2008 (now part of Code on Occupational Safety, Health and Working Conditions Code, 2020) provides for registration of these workers. As per the objects and reasons, 93% or more of Indians are in this sector.

There is a distinction between the terms 'unorganized workers' and 'unorganized sector workers' as these terms have not been precisely used. Trade Unions are organizations of workers. So, when we normally refer to 'organized workers' we may think of them as members of trade unions while those who are not grouped into trade unions as unorganized. We might even say that workers are highly organized in such and such an industry and less so in others. However, this is not how the term has been used in the statute – so unorganized workers are in effect unorganized sector workers.

Further, once unorganized sector workers are registered the difference between organized/unorganized may blur. Another way to think of organized workers is to look at the social security legislation that applies to them (such as Health Insurance and Provident Fund related provisions). Unorganized sector workers have been outside the purview of these laws so far. Hence, a new enactment was needed for them.

A. Vulnerable Groups

The 'wealth of a nation'[xi] depends on a healthy and productive workforce. However, not everyone is able to participate in manufacturing or other productive occupations. An appropriate use of technology and automation can help vulnerable sections of the society do more with their efforts. For example, a frail woman can operate heavy machinery by learning the technology involved. She can accomplish more in a day than what many able bodied workers can do using lower level technology.

The Ministry of Labour and Employment refers to vulnerable groups such as women, children, unorganized sector workers etc. and the State interventions that cater to the needs of that group. These include children, adolescents, women, pregnant women, and members of SC/ST community, migrants, contract workers, disabled or differently abled, unorganized sector workers, unemployed, apprentices and others. Various labour laws are designed to benefit such groups of workers [2][3].

B. Work arrangements

Different types of work arrangements are not defined in legislation or some of them may be defined but not so uniformly in different laws.

Apprentice: A person in certain designated trades can work as a trade apprentice. Similarly, technical and engineering degree holders or students can work as apprentices in certain establishments for a period of time.

Full time: Here a person can work for the normal length of the workday which may be 8 hours. However, ILO norms set upper limits on the total number of weekly work hours which many countries may adopt.

Part time: There is greater room for this type of part-time engagement to be created in the formal economy. Well-designed part time options can increase the available pool of work opportunities. More people do the work within the business at different times. Part time work may be especially suitable for women who may have to balance housework and childcare with career goals in some Indian families.

Temporary work: This is a work engagement for a short duration of time say a few weeks or months, or even years.

Fixed Term Employment: This is a type of temporary work of a fixed tenure of say a few years instead of a life-long permanent job and has recently been encouraged by the Government.

Intermittent work: In some provisions of labour laws, intermittent work is described as 'free time' during regular working hours that doesn't require attention or effort.

Seasonal work: Here work may repeat over years during certain months of the year such as summer employment.

Casual work: This is a type of informal work arrangement in which the terms of employment are probably implied rather than formally listed out.

The word casual can also be inferred from its usage in other laws. This is a type of employment arrangement which is not fully formalized yet.

Table 2.5 - Legal aspects related to arrangement of work.

• Apprentice is a broader term and can include apprentices other than those defined under Apprentices Act, 1961. S. 18 of the Act clearly mentions that appren-

tices are not workers.

- In India, Factories Act provisions of The Occupational Safety, Health and Working Conditions Code, 2020 prescribes period of work and breaks. Ordinarily no worker is allowed to work beyond 8 hours in a day in any establishment. Any additional work would be deemed to be overtime work.
- As per S. 13(3) of the Code on Wages Act, 2019, this is defined as work that may involve periods not having any physical activity or requiring sustained attention.
- In S. 45 (2) explanation to the proviso, of the Contract Labour provisions of The Occupational Safety, Health and Working Conditions Code, 2020, if work is performed for more than 120 days it is deemed as **not intermittent**. Also, if seasonal work is performed for more than 60 days in a preceding year it is considered **not intermittent**.
- Industrial Relations Code, 2020, S. 65 mentions work of a seasonal or intermittent nature although these are not defined in the Act clearly.
- Industrial Relations Code, 2020, clarifies that a *badli* or casual workman is someone whose name may not be borne on the muster rolls of the industrial establishment.
- S. 67 of Industrial Relations Code, 2020 explains Badli workman as someone who is employed in place of another who is probably a regular. (Badli could literally mean 'changed in place of'). A person who has finished one year as Badli is then considered a regular employee.
- Casual vacancy is described in Equal Remuneration Rules (now amalgamated into the Code on Wages, 2019 and the Code on Wages Rules, 2020). In explaining how the members of the Board have to be appointed the contingency of sudden vacancies are described. So, often a casual vacancy arises in the position of a regular member

of the Board. This vacancy is often filled up on an immediate and ad hoc basis till another regular member is found.

C. Nature of work or types of workers

We can refer to the relevant Statutes and examine the types of work mentioned in the definitions.

The Code on Wages Act, 2019 provides for fixing of minimum rates of wages for all employments. These workers may be skilled or unskilled, manual or clerical.

The Occupational Safety, Health and Working Conditions Code, 2020 lists the following types of workers. Similar lists are provided by most other labour laws. It may be helpful to understand them:

1. Manual
2. Unskilled
3. Skilled
4. Technical
5. Operational
6. Clerical
7. Supervisory

Three other types of work are mentioned, and these are generally excluded

8. Apprentice (as defined in 2(aa) of Apprentices Act, 1961)
9. Administrative
10. Managerial

The Industrial Relations Code, 2020, provides for Model Standing Orders. In new establishments that are large in size wherein it doesn't have its own Certified Standing Orders, then these model orders will be applicable as a default. Classification of workers is provided under Model Standing Orders. This classification can serve as a rough starting point to understand various types of workers in Indian establishments.

The Ministry of Labour and Employment is working on further clarifying these types of work. Model Standing Orders are being developed that provide some direction in this regard. The Code on Wages Rules, 2020 also attempted to simplify these terms.

As per Industrial Employment Standing Orders (Central Rules), 1946; in Schedule I the following are mentioned:

- Permanent
- Probationers
- Badli
- Temporary
- Casual
- Apprentices

These are further explained in the Model Standing Orders.

We can closely examine a few of the terms:

Unskilled – Work is performed that doesn't require mastering of any set of tasks or actions performed in a certain order. Any able-bodied person can take up such works and hence this is called unskilled work. The Mahatma Gandhi National Rural Employment Guarantee Act, 2005 defines 'unskilled manual work'. 'Any physical work which any adult person is capable of doing without any skill or special training' is considered to be unskilled manual work.

Semi-skilled workers may perform work of the kind that may require the possession of certain skills.

Similarly, other types of workers such as Skilled, Technical, Clerical can be understood.

A brief insight into Supervisory, Administrative, and Managerial work can be gained by studying the Industrial Relations Code,

2020.

In the Code of Wages Act, 2019, a person earning more than INR 15,000 p.m. (or another amount as notified/amended from time to time) and engaged in work of a supervisory nature would **not** be considered as a workman. This amount in the Industrial Relations Code, 2020 is INR 20,000 p.m. So, all supervisor below this **wage ceiling** would be considered workers. Also, a person in a managerial or administrative role would not be considered a workman.

The Industrial Relations Code, 2020 excludes apprentices under Apprentices Act, 1961. S. 18 of Apprentices Act, 1961 too clarifies that apprentices are trainees and not workers. Under Model Standing Orders, an apprentice is a learner who is paid an allowance during the period of his training.

Chapter Notes

6. The *Navaratna* and *Maharatna* companies are formidable in their size and contribution to the country. They have demonstrated that they can compete well with the private sector, and they provide employment and training opportunities to many Indians. More on them at dpe.gov.in

7. Post 1991, the acceleration of job creation in PSUs was reduced as per some reports.

8. When the number of vacancies is lower than the number of job seekers – some are not placed at the end of the year. If this continues, it has a cumulative effect over the years.

9. Some reports indicate that organized sector jobs have not increased substantially.

10. Based on NSSO surveys of 2009-10; these figures were used by the Ministry of Labour and Employment.

11. One way to think of how the labour laws are designed is to

examine if everyone can contribute towards growth.

Recent Developments – A real life scenario

IR managers play an important role in the public sector and in various government undertakings. The question of reservations often comes up in public employment.

Government of India Rules for reservations in employment for members of SC, ST, OBC, and women workers would be of interest to IR managers. There are also rules for disabled or 'differently-abled' citizens. A separate Act provides for accommodation to the disabled and has clear implications for workplace decisions.

While reservations for OBCs was contested a few decades back, now communities are seeking to be listed as an OBC in order to benefit from the reservation policies.

New categories have also been added that require protection such as sexual minorities (LGBTQ+) and EWS (Economically Weaker Sections) among the general classes.

Sources: Derived after reading several articles published in the Times of India, Deccan Chronicle, and The Hindu during 2017-18.

CHAPTER 3

Recruitment and Selection

"Simply complying with Equal Remuneration Provisions of the Code of Wages Act, 2019, can truly transform the already formidable business sector of India. Government, public, and social sectors can gain too."

Employers

Amul is preparing for an upcoming interview with his friends. He asks, "When people look for jobs, they must work somewhere. What is the range of options of where they seek work?"

Gita explains, "From a labour law standpoint, *establishment* is the term used to describe companies or businesses that are covered under various enactments.

The term 'appropriate Government' is used to refer either to the Central Government or the State Government that is responsible for implementing provisions with respect to the establishment concerned. Usually entities that are under the control of the Central Government will have the Central Government as the appropriate government."

Amul, "'Hmm... So how many establishments exist in India?"

Gita, "In a large country such as India you have many establishments[xii]. Some terms have statutory meaning – that is they are defined under the respective Statute. So, a Factory may mean an establishment defined as a factory under the relevant statute. Similar meanings can be attached to Mines, Plantations, and Shops and Establishments. Film workers, newspaper workers, building and other construction workers, and dock workers are other groups/industries that have specific enactments".

Table 3.1 - Legal aspects related to number of employees.

- Very small establishments are those having 1 to 9 employees. Small establishments are those having 10-40 employees. These definitions are provided in Labour Laws (Simplification of Procedure for Furnishing Returns and Maintaining Registers by Certain Establishments) Act, 1988.
- There is a lack of uniformity over other **number threshold** though. Provident Fund provisions apply to establishments having 20 or more workers. Other benefits such as Gratuity is applicable to establishments with 10 or more workers. Standing Orders provisions apply in Industrial Relations Code, 2020 to establishments having 300 or more workers.
- A list of applicability of Acts based on headcount increases can be created. Some provisions would apply only when the number of workers equals or exceeds a certain number. For example, canteen facility may need to be provided if the number of workers in an establishment including contract workers equals or exceeds 100. This is mentioned in S. 24 (v) of The Occupational Safety, Health and Working Conditions Code, 2020.

Job Application

Amul, "The search for work begins with a job application. This means, work is offered only to those who want it. Many people may choose to be idle. There is nothing the matter with this per se. However, different communities view idleness differently. People believe that continued idleness can weaken a person, family, or community financially. Government can help citizens from its tax revenue. However, this depends on the ability to pay taxes by individuals, households, and businesses. This in turn depends on the growth of the economy."

Gita, "Sure, it is pretty circular and complicated. Anyway, let's talk about applying for jobs. Indian law doesn't stipulate a format for a cover letter or a job application form that applies uniformly across the country. Shops and Establishment Acts of individual states may have a specific format for jobs in Shops and Establishments. Usually it is helpful to follow the format provided by the employer as information requirements change from one type of organization or one industry to another."

Recruitment and Selection

This is an important process that can determine if a job works out. However, one must be sensitive to issues of discrimination here. Men and women must be treated equally. So, if Amul and Gita were to apply for the same job, one candidate must not be picked over the other because of gender. Such practices are prohibited by Code of Wages Act, 2019. Of course, there may be certain jobs in specific occupations that may require those jobs to be given to men only – in which case it is not deemed to be discriminatory by definition.

Recruitment activities must provide the widest possible publicity to all possible qualified candidates. However, there would be practical considerations of costs and logistics for any business. So, they may choose to place their advertisements only in certain outlets or to a limited section of its target population.

We assume that having a job is the same as having a permanent and possibly life-time employment with an organization. In present times this view is being questioned. A whole range of employment opportunities exist that may work to the advantage of both the business and the jobseeker. Exploring alternative work arrangements such as part time work, contract opportunities, temporary roles etc. is central to addressing employment related challenges. Fixed term contracts have been proposed by the Central Government (apparently these worked well in the textile sector) as a simple arrangement to boost employment.

Apprenticeship

Amul, "Employers are not hiring because they are not finding the person with the right skills! So, should we not encourage apprenticeship?"

Gita, "Yes. Let me tell you what I know about it. A young person of 14 can begin to develop practical skills in a chosen trade, technology or engineering field. She or he can enter a contract of apprenticeship in a designated trade or technology field with an employer who can offer good training. Post training, based on the contract terms, an apprentice may or may not be required to work for the business.

Properly implemented, this can provide the much-needed industrial experience and practical know-how in key technology and engineering subjects. The nominal stipend amount (Government may share the stipend amount) paid by employer for technician or a graduate trainee is also good for employers – they can keep costs low while training and developing suitable manpower who may eventually become employees.

Through the functioning of Apprenticeship Advisers and through stipulations of the number of trainee posts in designated trades or technical areas, the Government can control and regulate this aspect of the labour market. In other words, the law empowers the Government officer to deal with training in public and private establishments and possibly initial placement (if employer is satisfied).

It is also possible to be an apprentice in general and not through the specific scheme envisaged by Apprentices Act, 1961, alone. While this is possible, the control and regulation of the relationship (and what to do in case it goes sour) does not exist. There is no compulsion or incentive for a business to simply take up apprentices on their own initiative."

Career Centers

Amul's next question, "Businesses in India were required to inform employment exchanges earlier. Nowadays they have to notify Career Centers of job vacancies created within their organizations. So, is it possible for someone to do an online search of jobs of her interest?"

Gita, "Yes, I think such technology-based solutions can help the person find a suitable job. On the other hand, for companies, Career Centers are good recruitment tools. However, for selection, businesses are not obliged to hire job seekers identified by the exchange."

Table 3.2 - Legal aspects related to women workers.

Code of Wages Act, 2019
• Some provisions relate to Equal pay for equal work and non-discrimination in hiring and other job processes between men and women are included in this Act.
• The Code on Wages, 2019 provisions are about non-discrimination based on gender. Also, advisory committees would be set up that will increase employment opportunities for women including part-time opportunities.

Other types of discrimination

Gita goes on to explain other types of discrimination:

"Constitution provides for affirmative action and equal opportunity. Region, religion, class, and other divisions exist in India which is one of the largest and most populous countries in the world today. Articles in the Constitution are general and apply to public employment opportunities. The government usually enacts legislation to convert these into workable provisions and rules, with enforcement machinery. This has happened in the case of women through Equal Remuneration Act, 1976 which is now amalgamated into the Code on Wages Act, 2019, which gives effect to one of the Directive Principles of State Policy.

In many cases, such specificity may not be available. However, it is good to adhere to general principles of equal opportunity in private employment although rules may not be specified in a precise manner for every possible scenario.

Harassment and restrictions on women

Any type of harassment or seeking of favors in return for providing employment is considered inappropriate. In the last few years, a law was passed to prevent harassment at the workplace. These laws also impact workplace decisions although they are not specific enactments under the Ministry of Labour. Restrictions placed on women (such as confinement during periods) has been deemed illegal in Nepal in 2017[xiii] which is culturally similar to India".

Nepotism, favoritism, and other unethical practices

Amul, "Okay, what other aspects must an ideal employer keep in mind?"

Gita, "Other unethical practices that impinge on the principle of equal opportunity exist such as nepotism (preferring one's family members and relatives for public employment) and favoritism (choosing friends over the best candidate for a job); while the specifics of many such cases may not be laid down in law, such practices are best avoided. Legal remedies may exist for affected parties which may or may not be pursued by either party to higher levels of the judiciary.

Starting a new business may require help from family, relatives, or friends. Such fund-raising activities create jobs in the private sector while absorbing business risks and are generally not considered by the Government to be nepotism or favoritism as such. These matters come under the subject of family business or entrepreneurship and not labour law or employment for wages/salaries.

We in India believe that our country is a free and democratic one. Indian citizens can socially interact with family members, relatives, friends and contacts both within and outside the country. Through these interactions they may gain socially or economically either through gifts or other benefits in cash or kind. All these activities are outside the context of wage employment. Hence, they do not fall under the purview of employment law as such.

Many Indian citizens may choose to invest in businesses or travel and work abroad with the help of near and dear. Some others may find prosperity through engagement in a community or social organization in addition to or apart from the workplace. The employer, the trade union, and the appropriate government are but only three of the entities in the worker's overall interactions with organizations (although arguably the three most important ones). And this limited set is the subject of Employment law and industrial relations. Our limited concern is the worker's engagement with an establishment registered in India. In global terms, this itself is pretty big given the size of the 'organized workforce' (although a small percentage of total workforce) in our part of the world."

Table 3.3 - Legal aspects related to international workers.

• Specific laws exist related to emigrants travelling abroad for work. These are not part of the Central labour laws as such. However, the issues of migrants may be handled by other Ministries in the Union Government dealing with overseas Indians and foreign governments. • Similarly, expatriate workers are now becoming common. Managers may need to engage foreign workers in India and the laws related to employment of such foreign workers is again not part of Central labour laws, but these can be studied further from the relevant Ministry of the Union Government. Normally, the Ministry of Home Affairs deals with these subjects. • Recently, a return in the form IW-1 related to Provident Fund is being sought from employers of international workers. Eventually these aspects may be covered by the provident fund provisions within The Code on Social Security, 2020.

Chapter Notes

1. There has been no systematic study of various types of organizations in India. Organizations doing similar type of work can be registered under different Acts.

2. The Times of India reported on developments in Nepal.

Recent Developments – Real life scenario

Charging of application fees from candidates seeking employment has become a common practice in many companies. Although, this is not essential, it can help in filtering out the less serious candidates. The Central labour laws have been silent on these practices.

The execution of an employment bond for good conduct with a certain surety amount is also being practiced by some companies. IR managers must weigh the relative advantages and disadvantages of these types of practices. The Central labour laws have been silent on such procedures. These instruments would be covered under Civil laws such as the law of contracts.

Sources: Several articles published in the Times of India, Deccan Chronicle, and The Hindu during 2017-18.

PART II: GETTING AHEAD

CHAPTER 4

Progressing in the job

"There is a lot one can do for one's own career to get ahead."

Rajesh did well in the interview and got the offer letter. He accepts the offer of employment. Later, he received the appointment order listing out the terms and conditions of work.

Shwetha reads this. "The duties and responsibilities are listed out in the communication from the company. I am studying this carefully. Usually, the terms and conditions will be derived from the Standing Orders for workers. For managerial work the employment terms and conditions can differ and often may be more favorable in terms of working time, facilities and privileges, and other compensation features. This is because the Standing Orders do not apply to excluded workers as defined by the legislation related to industrial disputes. Managers and administrators are not covered and so too supervisory employees drawing above a certain threshold."

Remuneration differences

Shwetha says, "So are you going to be one of the better paid employees?"

Rajesh, "In socialist countries, the workers may expect the managers to 'lead from the front' and follow the same timings, uniform, length of tenure, and commitment to the company or organization. Such views are becoming unrealistic, though. Further, full equality has not been achieved in Marxist countries and Western critics have called the managers and leaders of these countries 'state capitalists'.

What this really means, in a rather cynical way, is that the managers within the public sector and government undertakings in Socialist countries operate in very similar manner as business heads of private enterprises in Western democracies do. In socialist countries, these leaders are supposed to work for the 'State' and in Western democracies they ought to work for 'shareholders gains'. All said and done, their lifestyle and work approach and owner-agent conflicts have some parallels. Anyway, I do think I should be paid more. And I don't have to wear a uniform like the other workers every day."

The rise of the managerial cadre

Rajesh goes on to explain, "Around the world, a new *managerial cadre* has emerged. Hundreds of thousands of these managers are now working for MNCs and are employed all over the world. Many of them may have taken the GMAT examination after graduation and studied management in the US or Europe. These managers and business leaders continue to enjoy perks and privileges that are unimaginable for many labourers or wage earners. These highfliers may work for a business only for a few years and hop jobs for higher pay. Later in their life, they may take up international assignments or change careers or start their own ventures. During their working lives they may take vacations travelling to island destinations or other 'happening places'. So, I guess I will be treated differently."

Progressing for the Indian worker

Shwetha, "Okay, but can a poor Indian citizen aspire for a better life?"

Rajesh, "Well, employment is only one of the ways in which a person can progress. There are other ways through which a person can make money such as selling assets after they appreciate in value, renting out equipment or a built-up area, or one can gain through providing petty services, trading, or earning commissions etc. But for a poor person, income gained from laboring in the fields or factories is probably the easiest and simplest way forward. However, to enter the world of work and to contribute and gain from it, there are certain rules and norms."

Shwetha, "Yes, and let me tell you what they could be."

Finding out which laws apply to a particular worker

It is fair to assume that Indian workers are not familiar with which laws apply to them. Although school education in India provides for a basic coverage of Fundamental Rights and Duties in a civics course– this level of education is by and large not enough to deal with the complexities of industrial life.

Usually the worker, coming from a rural or semi-urban background, is suddenly confronted with the modern organization – a dynamic and complex international system involving advanced technological tools developed in distant and powerful countries applied with military precision on him and his family here in India. Unless this modern and powerful system is benevolent and caring – the Indian worker stands no chance whatsoever. His hopes and aspirations can be crushed in no time and he may be smashed out of the world of work and disappear into oblivion.

The condition of women workers and other vulnerable groups is still worse. There is absolutely no way that they can aspire to succeed in the modern workplace. These groups need to convince managers in the companies they work for that it is indeed worthwhile to invest time and money in them. Their behaviour must be impeccable and appropriate for the modern workplace so that it does not create any difficulties in the working of the business. Learning these skills may itself take several years for many – an advantage in life already gained by the well to do through good schooling. Any confrontationist approach would prove devastating to the member of the vulnerable group vis-a-vis the employer.

In order to balance this toxic situation, employers are required by law to display labour laws and rules in a language that most workers are familiar with usually at or near the entrance of the factory or establishment. If employers do make these details available and some or many workers see them, they may slowly become aware of their rights.

The government too has taken initiatives through worker education schemes[xiv]. Heroic as these efforts may be – it is important to recognize that most Indians are basically illiterate. Many who are educated can be considered as being 'functionally illiterate' – they cannot practically use their linguistic powers to interact with the world and get what they are entitled to. Further, many more have 'domain specific illiteracies' – they may be unaware of the welfare laws applicable to them and the mode of securing the benefits."

Rajesh, "True. So, what can Indian workers do to get ahead?"

Shwetha, "Well, I think there are some basic deficiencies that he has to overcome. The labourer starts off with a low base. If he or she belongs to a vulnerable group – member of SC/ST community, a woman, or a person from a poor family he or she is already behind in the race to greater wealth. A poor constitution is probably the biggest disadvantage she has. Continued ill-health during one's life is another factor. Access to clean drinking water and nutritious food can make some difference, though.

However, his or her social relationships are what we must examine. Here, she may be influenced by various types of addictions – notable among these is addiction to tobacco. Addiction to alcoholic drinks and exposure to narcotic substances would certainly be disastrous. Abusive family ties and a violent or unsafe neighborhood can make matters worse. Poor managerial or supervisory skills of the foremen and other authorities at work can play havoc with any chances of progress."

Rajesh, "But are we not getting too preachy in terms of telling the worker what to drink and what not to drink?"

Swetha, "Well, I am merely looking at the conditions from the standpoint of productive efficiency and factors responsible for poverty. These conditions are applicable to a large section of workers and are descriptive of their situation and predictive of their future. Further, they are competing with individuals from around the world many of whom are already millionaires or billionaires, progressing daily and strengthening their social and family bonds further. How can these workers with their weaknesses, addictions, and poverty ever overtake them? The workers may choose to cooperate with successful businesses but who knows what the terms of that cooperation would be."

Difference between school and work

Rajesh, "You are probably right. We need to also think about the work itself. For most labourers and wage earners, the key question is how does one become a good employee? Here if we understand the nature of working relationships in contrast with say other social or cultural relationships we can dwell on the concept of effective versus ineffective behaviour.

Work relationships are built on assignments. A project is usually broken down into smaller units. Similarly, a bigger task is divided into smaller tasks and assigned to employees. So, doing the work assigned to oneself is essential to building a good work relationship. Similarly, there must be a good professional relationship with the work team and supervisor.

Also, organizational citizenship norms such as those relating to workplace behaviors must be adhered to for success at work. This may involve workplace etiquette, meeting deadlines, being sensitive and responding appropriately to various developments at work, interacting in a socially appropriate manner with work associates and so on."

Progressing for apprentices

Swetha, "All these seem to be coming out of your own little head. People may disagree with you."

Rajesh, "Yes, while none of the above is specifically laid down in law, we find an allusion to this in the relevant laws."

Table 4.1 -Legal aspects related to expected behaviors of employee or worker.

• Apprentices Act, 1961 - under Sec 12 apprentices are obliged to attend classes regularly, carry out lawful orders of employer, and carry out other obligations as per contract. Similarly, an employer under Section 11 is expected to carry out his obligations as per contract.
• Details of expected behaviors are also spelt out in the Apprenticeship contract as provided in the Central Apprentices Rules.
• In the Industrial Relations Code, 2020 in the Second Schedule, a list is provided of unfair practices. Under Trade Unions provisions of the Industrial Relations Code, 2020, too we see an allusion to this in relation to unfair labour and trade practices. The immunities available to office bearers of trade unions also have certain limitations.
• For example, riotous and disorderly conduct is iden-

tified in the laws and costs are imposed on workers who engage in such behaviour and they may be disentitled to benefits under the Payment of Bonus chapter of the Code on Wages Act, 2019.

- Similarly, in the Code on Social Security, 2020, S. 41(3) clarifies that workers are expected to follow medical instructions. Failure to respond to safety instructions can also make workers ineligible for benefits under the S. 74 of the Act.

Progressing for workers in general

Rajesh goes on to explain in detail, "The Indian Constitution doesn't envisage violent acts by citizens. All citizens are expected to behave as ideal citizens. The Fundamental Duties provide a guide to appropriate behaviour expected of Indian citizens although they may not be enforceable in the Courts. The historical background of when these were included in the Constitution through an amendment obfuscates their status. However, the message seems to be that certain basic behaviors can be expected from all citizens by the State.

In practice, we see a wide deviation from the expected norms of behaviour given individual circumstances, education and social conditions and other factors playing a role. A cross country comparison can reveal how Indians compare with say German or Canadian workers. Within-country studies can also reveal how Indian workers behave across regions and industries.

This basic feature of an 'expectation' of good behaviour on the part of the citizens can also be taken to the industrial setting. Here certain behaviors are expected of workers. Failure to engage in them may disentitle them to benefits under various labour laws."

General guidelines for winning at work

Dheeraj, a TU leader, thinks of a set of guidelines for new workers in the factory that can help them be more effective.

Dheeraj lists out what he thinks:

Workers must first attempt to organize themselves. This may involve joining a trade union or working with a legal representative. Unionism itself is restricted in some countries of the world. However, workers may have access to legal help in such countries and they may be more educated and aware of their rights. In India, it is helpful for many workers to join trade unions and share their concerns and problems with union members or officials.

Becoming Aware

1. Identify which labour laws apply to you. A good place to start is from where they are posted or displayed in the establishment. Even if a person is in an administrative or managerial role, some laws would apply. Become a member of a trade union[xv] or get the services of a legal practitioner who can assist you. At the very least, a person must be able to enlist the services of a legal representative.

2. Ascertain if the organization is covered under those statutes. Some establishments may be exempt. Certain laws apply when employees exceed a certain number within the establishment. The nature of business may exclude them from the application of a particular Act.

3. Understand the benefits available under the Act and the eligibility criteria for those benefits. The terms and conditions of employment and the attendance

and leave rules are relevant too.

4. Recognize who the employer is, the enforcement and appellate authorities under the Act, and the appropriate Government (it could be the State or Central Government).

5. Exercise choice of making any contribution to a Fund established under the Act after learning about the same. Often the law requires enrolment into a scheme immediately upon joining - in which case the worker may learn about the scheme in due course of time.

Table 4.2 - Legal aspects related to workers benefits

- As per the Code on Wages Act, 2019 S. 52, complaints can only be made by authorized officers or organizations, employees or a registered Trade Union. The role of social welfare organizations as in the case of the now repealed Equal Remuneration Act, 1976 has not been mentioned.

- In some Acts, a person must be employed for at least 240 days in a year to be deemed as someone in continuous service.

Understanding wages or salary

1. Making suitable and appropriate nominations is important. In some cases, nominees must come from the members of the family. It is important to understand who the family is from a legal standpoint. In some cases, the employee may acquire the family after joining work. The worker may be required to intimate the HR department about this.

2. The definition of what a *wage* has been made similar in all Acts. The various components of wages may have to be examined. Some of which may be cash value of the benefit that is provided in kind. Some service or other amenities may be provided whose monetary value may be ascertained and made a part of the wages or salary. With consolidation of various Acts into the four codes, the definition of wage is now uniform in all codes.

3. Understand overtime rates and its application to oneself. This means understanding the normal working hours in the factory or establishment and the eligibility for an overtime rate of work if performed beyond regular hours.

4. Understand what continuous service is under various laws.

5. Protected benefits are provided by the labour laws. In other words, the earnings are protected from civil or criminal proceedings and not liable to attachment.

6. Double benefits under different Central laws are generally avoided by provisions specifically listing them out. With the consolidation of Acts, those earlier provisions are less relevant now.

7. Better benefits may already be available to a worker beyond what is mentioned in the related statute. In such cases, the mutual agreement between the employer and employee is more salient and good.

Working with enforcement officials and dispute resolution machinery

1. Cooperate with inspectors or other enforcement officers and respond to any questions or provide any information sought in an appropriate manner.

2. Familiarize with the procedures involved in dealing with disputes, and the process of appeal in case one is given an adverse decision. In many cases authorities under the Act can be approached directly for immediate help without necessarily going in for adjudication.

3. Who is the appellant authority and the timeframe within which the decision can be appealed?

4. Know about the dispute resolution officials and mechanisms. The conciliation process, Industrial Tribunal, and National Industrial Tribunal is relevant here.

Recent Developments – A real life scenario

Whether 'industrial relations' covers clashes between local police and protestors in a city? In many parts of the world, residents of a city or town may be opposed to the setting up of a factory in the vicinity of a residential area. Since employees of the establishment or other establishments in the same industry are not directly involved in these conflicts - this may not be a pure case of industrial relations.

The conflict appears to be between the members of the general public or residents of a particular area and the factory. IR managers would normally be alert to such developments.

Sources: Several articles published in the Times of India, Deccan Chronicle, and The Hindu during 2017-18.

CHAPTER 5

You and the personnel department

"A meticulous implementation of labour laws by establishments can transform hundreds of millions of lives."

Rajesh has finished his first year at work. He goes to meet his boss Mr. Vikram. His boss wants Rajesh to assist him in developing a program for improving the performance of IR managers.

Rajesh says, "Here is what I think. During their work, employees will be interacting with the HR or Personnel department. The person one may meet could be a labour welfare officer, the personnel officer or the manager of a department.

Most people don't know what the Employee Relations department does as part of its work. Employee Relations managers have certain constraints imposed by law. They also have certain choices they can make to increase opportunities and attract qualified and competent workers."

Mr. Vikram, "Okay, can you do the homework and come back next week?"

Rajesh studies the laws and his notes from college and draws up a set of implications, some general and some specific to each Act:

General implications for IR managers:

- Each of the Acts probably has certain requirements of maintaining registers. For small and very small establishments, these requirements may be reduced. It is helpful to know what these returns, notifications, or registers are and how they should be maintained.
- The period of continuous work is often lesser for seasonal establishments. Also, the quantum of benefit may be lesser too.
- It is important to be thoroughly familiar with the appeal process. The employee may initiate this process by appealing against the decision of a controlling authority or an enforcement officer. The employer may have to respond within a certain period or appear before the appellant authority.
- Most Acts clarify how offences by companies must be handled. Usually, every person who is responsible for and in-charge of the conduct of the business of the company as well as the company are deemed to be guilty. Senior officials may have to prove that they were unaware or exercised due diligence to prevent the commission of the offence.
- Certain laws may require contributions to be deducted from the employee's salary such as Employees' Provident Funds and Miscellaneous Provisions Act, 1952 and Employees' State Insurance Act, 1948. Now these Acts are part of the Code on Social Security, 2020. These payments then go into a Fund and the monies from it may be utilized to provide social security benefits.

Rajesh presents his report to Mr. Vikram.

Mr. Vikram, "Okay, this looks good. But is that all?"

Rajesh, "I have not covered every aspect of each of the Acts. In labour law, one must finally go to the full text of the enactment and the subordinate legislation. Also, all labour laws in the Union Ministry are not covered. But I covered many of the important ones."

Mr. Vikram, "I think this is a very good beginning. Please organize a meeting with the relevant managers from various plants."

Recent Developments – A real life scenario

A sudden explosion in a factory killed 7 people and injured many others. Rajesh was the new Employee Relations Manager.

Rajesh's super boss asks him to study the matter and inform about the steps the company should take. Meanwhile, she was also working on the same issue on a continuous basis with other colleagues and senior managers. Rajesh begins by examining what are his duties as laid down in the laws.

Sources: Several articles published in the Times of India, Deccan Chronicle, and The Hindu during 2017-18.

◆ ◆ ◆

PART III: STAYING AHEAD

CHAPTER 6

How is it elsewhere? Regional, national, and international aspects of IR

"State Governments have a substantial role to play."

Amul, Tanya, and Gita are back from their first interview. Now they discuss how it went. Tanya, "Friends, we have not focused on the State Governments. Some questions from the HR member of the panel were on Gujarat where the plants are located."

Amul, "I know. Here is what I think:

Industrial Relations is influenced by three parties:

1.   The employee and employees' organizations such as trade unions.
2.   The employer, employer associations, and influence groups.
3.   The governments at local, state or federal (central) level.

The engagement of an employee with an establishment becomes a multi-dimensional interaction. At an individual level, it is the contract or employment relationship which is the primary determinant of the behaviour of the two parties. In order to avoid exploitation or other abuses of power, the government may step in and provide certain guidelines. The State Government, Central Government with their enforceable laws and regulations and model rules and international bodies such as ILO with its conventions and recommendations influence this relationship."

Regional aspects

Gita, "So what can State Governments do to improve the conditions of workers in their states?"

Amul, "I think a lot is possible. We have to examine it in totality and as per each of the enactments."

Tanya, "Industrial relations are actively influenced by State Governments. Enactments such as Shops and Establishments Act may be particular to individual states. Depending upon the economy of a region within the country, unique labour issues may emerge. These are addressed by passing laws relevant to that class of workers or establishments. Central laws may already exist, and these may need to be further defined at the State level. This may involve passing State specific rules if permitted by the Act or adopting or modifying certain Model Rules specified under the Act to that State. State Governments may also issue orders or notifications extending the act or specifying certain schedules, amounts, or authorities as per the Act.

The enforcement machinery to bring the provisions to bear may need initiative from State Governments. The resources and manpower deployed may vary depending upon the priorities of various regional Governments.

The implementation of the Act would involve regular inspections, review of registers and records that are to be maintained under the Act, publication of reports, engagement of civil society in discussion and critique of Government initiatives and evaluation of progress, audit of various projects etc."

National Aspects

Gita, "Right. Let me also say a few words about the national aspects. The Union government with its Central laws is the prime body for addressing national level aspects of Industrial Relations. Trade Union Federations that exist at the national level are also key players. The linkages existing between trade union federations and political parties ensure that the views of the workers are represented and voiced in the Parliament.

Employer bodies at the national level are also active and influence Indian policy whether it relates to matters of trade and commerce, industrial licensing, labour legislation, and finance."

International aspects

Amul, "International Labour Organization or the ILO, which was set up in 1919, is one of the major bodies operating at an international level to address labour issues. In addition, there are international trade union federations that are influential."

The key players

Amul, "The three key players as mentioned earlier are the Government, the employee, and the employer.

The Government itself is a massive organization in India and an understanding of this entity is needed to understand the various undertakings, establishments and organizations.

Government includes:
- Central Government.
- State Government.
- Local Government (Panchayats and Urban Local Bodies)."

Recent Developments – A real life scenario

Sandip has taken up a job in a new city in the western part of the country where there is a lot of 'action' in terms of entrepreneurship, new business ideas, innovations, and general progress. However, he wakes up in the morning to learn that many migrant workers are leaving the state due to clashes between locals and migrants.

Apparently, a few migrants attacked locals the previous week. He wonders what is going on and meets with his colleagues at work to discuss.

Sources: Derived after reading several articles published in the Times of India, Deccan Chronicle, and The Hindu during 2017-18.

CHAPTER 7

Industrial relations in new and specific industries

"Notions of work and organization are being redefined. What would IR become?"

1. Information Technology Industry

Tanya, "I want to take up a job in the software sector."

Table 7.1 - Facts and Figures of industry developments in 2017.

- Layoffs have been common in 2017. There has been a freeze on pay hikes of the IT sector in many companies. Trade unions have not been active in this sector. We also notice that software engineers and other employees have been less than outspoken about the issues and problems faced within the IT industry.

- In August 2017, the employees of public sector banks went on a 1-day strike to protest government policies related to the banking sector.

2. Banking and Financial Services

Amul, "And if you are exploring the banking industry - Public Sector Banks (PSBs) have unions. Private Banks are known for their efficiency and innovation."

Tanya, "If I were given an opportunity, I would examine the working of private sector banks on the following parameters:

1. Brief description of work environment.
2. What are the major HR issues faced by employees?
3. Are employees aware of their rights and responsibilities? Benefits and privileges?
4. How are the demands of employees channelized?
5. Are these laws relevant and in use – The Code on Wages Act, 2019; the Code on Industrial Relations, 2020, and so on?
6. How are grievances addressed?
7. How are employee issues such as health, safety, and welfare of employees different in the banking sector?
8. Who are the various employees and what are their duties?
9. How are disputes addressed?"

Amul, "So you want to carry out a survey research?"

Other industries

Tanya, "Maybe. But why the banking sector alone, we could look at other industries too. I feel that the following is a list of industries where the working of Industrial Relations presents varying and unique challenges:

- Oil and Gas
- Support Services Sector
- Automobiles

- Infrastructure
- Pharmaceuticals
- Metals and mining
- Agro-processing, dairying and allied fields
- Electronics and Telecommunications."

Recent Developments – A real life scenario

Strikes by transportation companies that have an impact on the running of medium scale enterprises would be of interest to IR managers. Transportation workers may strike for various reasons demanding better compensation or facilities and amenities from State or Central Governments.

This may impact the business of medium scale enterprises who depend on the supply of goods including raw materials and transportation of semi-finished and finished goods. These developments would concern IR managers as they would be able to better understand the dynamics of what is happening.

Sources: Several articles published in the Times of India, Deccan Chronicle, and The Hindu during 2017-18.

CHAPTER 8

Case Scenarios

Vinita and Sarla are now flying to Kolkata to meet their aunt. Vinita must attend an interview. Sarla says, "So are you prepared for the interview with a foreign company? Why aren't more foreign companies coming to India? I like Japanese companies, they come up with cool products like robots!"

Vinita says, "One of the oft repeated arguments made by entrepreneurs and MNCs that want to do business in India is the difficulty of complying with the labour laws. Renowned economists and advisers have argued that Indian laws are outdated, burdensome, and complicated."

Sarla, "So why don't we just get rid of them? More growth leads to more jobs."

Vinita, "You are still in school and will learn later about the why of it. Generally, labour issues are tripartite in nature – the employer, the worker, and the government need to provide inputs. It would be unusual for a big company and the government to settle these matters among themselves easily.

I, therefore, say that whether 'progress' and societal improvement can indeed be gained through rapid economic growth is debatable; the rights of workers and the principles of basic dignity of human life, the right to work, and other such fundamentals are accepted by all business and political leaders all over the world. No economist or political theorist has been able to argue to the contrary in a convincing manner so far"

Sarla, "Really, how do you know?"

Vinita, "Just hear me out. It is safe to say that concepts related to basic worker rights have withstood the test of time and have wide acceptance across geographies. There are certainly unfortunate historical incidents and islands of authoritarianism even today where seemingly labour rights fade away. However, a number of these exceptions still do not make a rule. In other words, these counter-examples cannot provide a coherent and effective guide for action for IR students and business managers in a large country such as India."

Sarla, "Wow! that sounds almost philosophical. But why do you make such a spirited defense of the labour laws? Can we afford them?"

Vinita, "Many smart people have argued like you do. Financial advisors and economists often suggest 'reforms' or propose 'amendments' to bring about a certain result, a certain rate of growth etc. The Government on its own initiative amends these laws and has simplified them for small businesses recently. Sure, these suggestions on commercial viability cannot be interpreted as an attack on fundamental rights and basic freedoms of Indian citizens. These advisors are well-wishers and simply want us to be more prosperous. However, critics have argued that the rich benefit more from their genius.

That said, the most basic rights of citizens are already guaranteed in the Constitution. The rights of workers and employees also flow from its articles. One can infer that labour laws were enacted to further provide protection to workers from abuse or clumsiness by poorly trained managers. Sometimes, business owners too are driven by flawed ideologies or concepts. They may operate in ways that fails to meet international standards.

The term 'Labour laws' is a misnomer as it doesn't necessarily mean pro labour enactments wherein lazy people drain the profits of the heroic entrepreneur. I feel in many cases the Acts represent a tripartite settlement of sorts - for which costs and obligations are placed on both employers and employees. And of course, governments too have to strive toward maintaining labour standards."

Sarla, "But are these laws targeted at a particular country or company that wants to harm us?"

Vinita, "Not really. The laws were enacted not in response to a specific country or a specific MNC or MNCs wanting to enter India to sell their products. They evolved over time to help Indians, especially the vulnerable ones be protected by faulty business practices. They are meant to cover almost the whole of India and deal with different types of businesses and other organizations that already exist or may be set up in future by Indian or non-Indian entities that want their organizations to be registered in our country. The general idea seems to be to enlarge welfare benefits to as many Indian workers as possible. Usually some money is taken from the employee's pay. No special external help or aid is sought from foreign countries or wealthy philanthropists for these benefits. However, wealthy philanthropists can contribute to certain Funds or Schemes.

Neither are these laws targeted at any individual person whether Indian or non-Indian. In fact, most civilized people around the world would want these benefits to be available to their citizens. Often, they feel privileged and fortunate to be born in their country of birth or to be part of their country of adoption. Further, in their moments of prayer these individuals may hope that similar gifts are accessible more widely to people in other countries as well. If a certain nation were to withdraw these bare minimum facilities for its own citizens, that may lead to international outcry and condemnation! Let us see below what's the fuss all about regarding these labour laws:

- Vacancies to be notified so that job seekers can apply to them.
- Equal pay for women and non-discrimination of women at work.
- Hiring of apprentices.
- Timely payment of wages, usually monthly, and only specified deductions from pay.
- Minimum wages for certain occupations or in certain industries.
- Annual bonus payments for eligible workers.
- Payment of a gratuity amount after putting in say 5 years with an employer.
- Permitting working women to take up maternity or related processes.
- Sickness, maternity, compensation for injury, medical benefits, and funeral expenses for eligible employees.
- Compensation for death or disablement or injury during work.
- Government certified list of conditions of work.
- Allowing membership of a trade union that may have certain powers, functions and registration requirements.
- Resolution of industrial disputes through a resolution machinery and control of strikes, lockouts, retrenchment, closure, and other events.
- Health, welfare, safety, working conditions and related matters for factory workers.
- Facilities and protection of contract workers.
- Provident fund, pension, and insurance for certain workers.

And there are other laws too but since you are a kid, I don't want to trouble you with more. But you get the picture. Children too are protected by these laws. Now tell me. Who would not want these basic facilities for people working for our country and its industries whether public or private?"

Sarla, "Of course, I am not a bad girl! I want them too for our people. We don't need to be apologetic or embarrassed about our labour laws. We can even be proud that Indian citizens are benefitting overall. Genuine reform of the laws can still be welcome if more people benefit. Looks like you will impress in the interview."

Vinita, "Ok. High labour standards may actually improve the profile of the country. After all who would want to live in a country where:

- Vacancies are not notified.
- Women are discriminated against in an indiscriminate manner.
- No options exist for gaining skills in a engineering or trade area.
- Payments are not made in time.
- No standards exist for minimum pay.
- Pregnant women are forced to work, and pregnancy would work against them.
- If you are temporarily sick or injured, then it's all over for you.

And I could go on..."

Sarla, "Hell..., no! I wouldn't want to be part of such a bizarre and peculiar place. But my worry was only about affordability."

Vinita, "Thanks. Now in the cases below, the practical aspects of how Indian labour laws apply in specific circumstances is explored. This gives the reader a feel of which laws apply, and what are the practical considerations for an entrepreneur or business manager."

I. Gita - A Software Professional

Editorial Note: The Government is creating new Rules under the new Labour Code; some numbers and data mentioned below may have to be updated incorporating the most recent developments. These updated versions will be created from time to time.

Gita is an engineer and she got an offer through campus placement for a regular job. Her employer would have filed a return with the local employment exchange (now career center) before making an offer (the specifics of last date for applications would be specified in the Code on Social Security, 2020, Rules). Let us assume that she was offered a monthly pay of INR 30,000. If it was a public sector or Government owned organization the Government of India Rules in this regard for reservation would have applied.

Let us assume that she earlier worked as an apprentice. She was probably a graduate apprentice trainee. As per Rules under the Apprentices Act, 1961, she would get as a statutory amount a stipend. She would have got a slightly higher amount if she was working as a Sandwich course student for Degree. Most of the labour laws do not apply to Apprentices as per Apprentices Act, 1961, S. 18. The statutory stipend during apprenticeship training was probably informed by the provisions related to minimum wages as fixed by the appropriate Government. Higher pay is possible as per provisions of the Apprentices Act, 1961.

The question is whether the software sector is covered under the Code on Wages Act, 2019. Now that the Act applies to all establishments, it can be inferred that it applies to the Software Sector as well.

She can assume that principles of Equal Pay and non-discrimination as mentioned in the Code on Wages Act, 2019 was followed during the recruitment and selection processes. If a disproportionate number of male students were made an offer as compared to female students, a prima facie argument could be made that the provisions of the Act were violated. However, if the selection process was not biased as such and the difference in proportions of hires can be attributed to other reasonable causes other than the factor of sex, then this would not be an issue.

She can also expect from the employer, that transfer, and other HR decisions including promotions would not be discriminatory. She can aspire to reach the highest levels of the company if she works hard. She is thankful that she was born in India, studied here and now gets to work here. Let us assume that she was in a permanent job. If she was employed as a Fixed Term Employee, she will get all benefits up to a certain number of years. The Code on Wages, 2019 doesn't define Fixed Term Employees but other codes such Industrial Relations Code, 2020 and the Code on Social Security, 2020 do.

Minimum Wages provisions bring the concepts of time rate and piece rate of work. She may find similar concepts in place in describe highly skilled software work. Nevertheless, she doesn't have to worry about minimum wages as such. However, a number of office assistants, peons, and other helpers are working for the software company. She assures herself that they too are getting paid well. Thanks to the software industry, it has lifted many boats!

We assume that Payment of Wages provisions now apply to all wages and the previous wage ceilings have been removed as declared by the Government. Since she would be paid INR 30,000 p.m. the Act would apply to her. However, we need to look at the salary components to determine exactly what her wages are under the Act as per S. 2(y). Often employers club all different wage components and provide a CTC – Cost to Company amount. Also, a flexible cafeteria style benefits choice is provided by private employers where employees chose what is best for them and a 'smart salary package' is worked out which optimizes tax payments to GoI. So, idea being that it should appear that the employee is taking a good take home salary. However, from a legal standpoint an analysis is needed of her wages. For example, HRA

– House Rent Allowance, and CA – Conveyance Allowance are not part of wages as such. Further, the proviso to the wages definition states that the sum total of all remuneration that is calculated in S. 2(y)(a) to 2(y)(i) should not exceed 50% of wages; in case it does then the excess is included in the definition of wages. Anyway, she needs to understand the allowances and components of her salary. This will also allow her to compare her salary with her male colleagues to determine if she is getting her due. Also, if her wages are actually more than the wage ceiling for a worker under Industrial Relations Code, 2020 of INR 18,000 p.m. is something she should determine.

She can expect her salary to be given to her/electronically deposited as per S. 17(1)(iv) before the expiry of the 7th day of every month.

Payment of Bonus provisions would apply even if her salary is above a limit as notified by the appropriate Government. The wage ceiling amount would be used for calculating bonus as her salary of INR 30,000 p.m. would likely be above the wage ceiling. Earlier the eligibility ceiling was INR 21,000 p.m. notified in 2016 and w.e.f. 1.04.2014. The calculation limit was INR 7,000. These figures may be revised in the future as per price increases and increases in salary structure. Assuming that 20 or more employees are employed in her company, the provisions of Payment of Bonus would apply. We also assume that the company is actually providing services or manufacturing software. If the company is only in the process of building the product, then applicability of the provisions could be somewhat relaxed. Also, in the first few accounting years there is a relaxation on payment of bonus.

Nevertheless, she can still expect some gifts from her employer as part of Puja celebrations. Diwali is widely celebrated in India; similarly, Durga Puja is celebrated in some parts. Often commercial establishments give gifts to employees during this period. This is not a statutory bonus although payments can be adjusted against the statutory bonus for employees who are covered under the Act.

As per the Payment of Gratuity provisions (now part of The Code on Social Security, 2020), she would be eligible for gratuity if she finished at least 5 years with the company and her employment was terminated. The upper limit of how much gratuity she can receive was reviewed and increased recently. So, she can get a handsome amount from the employer (if her salary also increased over the years this could be substantial as 15 days' salary for every completed year would be calculated based on last drawn salary. Gratuity amount does have ceiling as notified from time to time). If she was a Fixed Term Employee, she would be eligible for gratuity at the end of her term at the same rate. However, the payment would be proportionately reduced as number of years served would be less. S. 53 clarifies that the eligibility period of 5 years would not be required for those who service expires on completion of fixed term employment.

The Occupational Safety, Health and Working Conditions Code, 2020 has provisions that describe restrictions and prohibitions on the working of women. As per S. 43, she may with her consent, be allowed to work in night shifts, that is, between 7 p.m. and 6 a.m. She may be prohibited from certain operations deemed to be dangerous and the appropriate Government may restrict her working on such assignments.

Although, she would like to become a member of a trade union, she probably would not find such an organization in the IT industry. However, she can socially interact with her work group and learn about the company and its procedures. Normally, if the company is getting a lot of business from certain parts of the world, it would try to comply with the cultural, managerial, and other norms of the country providing business. So, if trade unions are discouraged in certain countries, the IT industry may also discourage the same within India by working with and appealing to the State and Central Governments. Trade Unions provisions that are now part of the Industrial Relations Code, 2020 does apply to all establishments in India although trade unions may be less active in certain sectors and regions of India. Karnataka modified Standing Orders to permit greater freedom to the software sector.

A software company may not be deemed to be a factory under the Occupational Safety, Health and Working Conditions Code, 2020. This is because if the nature of work doesn't involve a manufacturing process as such then the establishment is not a factory. One could argue that employees are engaged in the production of software and hence a manufacturing activity is being undertaken. These matters may be decided by the authorities concerned based on the nature of business. Often, Shops and Establishments Act of individual states would cover various commercial establishments including technology and technical services companies.

Employees' State Insurance provisions in the Code on Social Security, 2020, would apply to establishments having 10 or more workers. Since, no notified hazardous or life-threatening work is underway at the business -in which case it would apply even for a single employee. Similarly, if her business is a notified business for Provident Fund provisions then these provisions would apply. As per Schedule I of the Code on Social Security, 2020, Provident Fund provisions will only apply to those establishments having 20 or more employees. As companies grow bigger and more influential, the government usually extends the benefits of the welfare statute to the employees of these companies. Also, in cases where employees are in receipt of benefits that are superior to what the law offers, often an exemption from the provisions of the law can be expected. In the software sector, she may be in receipt of benefits greater than what is provided in the relevant Acts for the manufacturing sector or for factories.

Maternity Benefit provisions (now part of the Code on Social Security, 2020) would apply and in case she wants to start a family or take up maternity (through adoption or other means), the law provides various benefits. She would be eligible for maternity leave, and other associated benefits. She can also expect that her conditions of employment would not be turned to her disadvantage because of the choices she would make.

Industrial Disputes provisions (now part of the Industrial Relations Code 2020) would apply to her. If she is in a supervisory capacity as a team leader of a software development team and as she is drawing salary above INR 18,000 p.m. (or a notified amount which may change from time to time) she would be excluded from the definition of a 'worker' and would be considered an employee instead. If she was doing work primarily of a technical or professional nature, she would be considered a **worker** and could raise an individual dispute for any adverse decisions such as dismissal or discharge against her.

Contract Labour provisions of the Occupational Safety, Health and Working Conditions Code, 2020, would apply if she was working for a contractor and deployed on a client site. However, if she was regularly being paid by the 'contractor' firm, then she would not be treated as such. Instead, she would be viewed as an employee of the 'contractor' firm.

Standing Orders provisions that are now part of Industrial Relations Code, 2020 would apply if the number of employees is 300 or more. This number is reduced in some states through amendments to the Act. She may have to check what applies in her State – say Karnataka or Maharashtra. However, if her salary is higher than INR 18,000 p.m. and she may not be deemed to be a 'worker' as per the definition in the Act if she is engaged in supervisory roles. This would mean that the Certified Standing Orders may not apply to her. What does this mean? It means that the number of rules related to classification of workers, identity badge, work timings, shifts, notice of change in shifts, prior notice of termination etc. would be different in her case. She should do well to refer to appointment order, other communications and agreements with higher ups in the company for these matters. In uncertain or general situations, it is usually helpful to be alert to the Standing Orders for workers but given her higher pay, the company may expect work of a higher order and greater commitment from her. She also has to do more than just the routine that is followed by many other workers.

Based on the above, several Acts would apply to her. As an engineer who has finished her undergraduate technology program, she probably doesn't understand the labour laws and how they work for her. A complex set of laws and various mechanisms are at play that is creating a workable environment for her to pursue her engineering dreams in the company of her choice.

There are other Acts too which may apply. There are more aspects to each of the Acts. However, the above case scenario is an illustration of how some of the provisions are relevant to her situation.

II. Raghuram returns to India

Raghuram returns to India to set up a company

Raghuram was living in the UK for many years and has now returned to India. He wants to set up a small firm. He wants to know if he and his team need to learn about labour laws

Raghuram is troubled by all the labour laws and thinks to himself, "Most of the problems faced by workers is because they are not getting paid well.

If a small business has a few employees and if all of them are well paid; do, we then need to worry about all the laws? The answer is yes and no. Many Acts have wage ceilings; so, they only apply to employees or workers that are paid below the amount. So, if all employees are well paid in a start-up, then they will all be above the wage ceiling. We don't need to then worry about these small welfare benefits. Right? Not really.

Usually, any business will have workers including unskilled office staff such as helper, office assistants and others. So, one must know about labour laws in order to appreciate the world of work. For example, laws are relevant irrespective of how much employees are being paid. Equal remuneration is an example.

Men and women should not be discriminated in pay and other HR decisions. This applies to same or work of a similar nature. The salary level is immaterial. So, this consideration of **equality** has to be given to men and women whether they are low paid unskilled workers. Or, if men and women are highly paid skilled workers even then **equality of pay** applies. Similarly, gratuity is a benefit to be paid on termination of employment (in regular employment it is after 5 years of work). This applies to both highly paid or low paid jobs. In Fixed Term Employment, gratuity may have to be paid sooner.

Examples of Acts that don't seem to have a wage ceiling as such:

1. Code on Social Security, 2020 provisions related to Employment Information and Monitoring. However, those employment drawing wages less than an amount as notified are excluded.
2. The Code on Wages Act, 2019 provisions related to Equal Pay.
3. Apprentices Act, 1961.
4. The Code on Wages Act, 2019 provisions related to Minimum Wages.
5. The Code on Social Security, 2020 (Payment of Gratuity provisions). Gratuity amount has a ceiling but there is no wage ceiling as such for eligibility.
6. The Code on Social Security, 2020 - Employees' Compensation related provisions.
7. Maternity Benefit related provisions within the Code on Social Security, 2020.
8. Factories Act provisions of the Occupational Safety,

Health and Working Conditions Code, 2020.
9. Trade Unions related provisions in the Industrial Relations Code, 2020.

Apprentices Act, 1961, doesn't have a wage ceiling. However, apprentices are usually paid a stipend that is usually less than regular amounts paid to workers in the establishment.

ESI provisions do have a wage ceiling however, managerial and supervisory employees may still be entitled to benefits such as insurance coverage.

The Maternity Benefit provisions too doesn't have a wage ceiling. The minimum wages applicable to a woman in The Code on Wages, 2019 will be used for ascertaining the wage threshold for her.

Factories Act, 1948, would apply if any manufacturing activity is going on and 10 or more workers are employed with the aid of power.

Labour Laws (Simplification of Procedure for Furnishing Returns and Maintaining Registers by Certain Establishments) Act, 1988 has substantially simplified the process for very small establishments having 1-9 employees and small establishments having 10-39 employees. All such establishments may need to only file an annual consolidated return in Form I and maintain registers in Form II and III for small and only Form III for very small establishments. However, this applies to only the 16 Central Labour Laws mentioned in Schedule I of the Act.

Below, let us look at each of the laws and examine how they apply to Raghuram's company.

1. To begin with, Raghuram should recognize that he has an establishment as per Code on Social Security, 2020 provisions related to Employment Information and Monitoring. He needs to report vacancies to a notified career center in a prescribed form and sub-

mit periodic returns.

2. He should not discriminate while hiring between men and women employees. Non-discrimination should extend to other HR decisions such as training and promotion. This is as per the Code on Wages Act, 2019.

3. Apprentices Act, 1961, may not apply to his establishment, as the Apprenticeship Adviser may deem the establishment to be new and small for imparting training. Smaller organizations may be asked to pool together to train apprentices and eventually if his establishment is in a designated trade he may be required to participate.

4. Payment of Wages provisions of the Code on Wages Act, 2019, would apply to his firm. He may be required to pay all employees their monthly pay before the expiry of the 7th day of the monthly period, if paid monthly. If other wage periods have been set, then they have other time periods before which payments have to be made. Other provisions such as fixing wage periods, maintaining registers or returns would apply too.

5. Provisions related to Minimum Wages of the Code on Wages Act, 2019, may not really apply to his establishment. In any case, he can ensure that all employees are paid above the minimum wage rate. Working hours are fixed, days of rest are fixed, and so on.

6. Payment of Bonus provisions of the Code on Wages Act, 2019, would apply only to workers drawing up to a certain notified amount. The Act would apply only if the number of employees exceed 20 and would continue to apply even if the number falls below the number during an accounting year. Also, in

the initial period when he is just beginning and not yet providing services or has not yet manufactured a product there is relaxation on payment of bonus. Even in the early years of his business he has certain relaxations during the first 5 accounting years especially if he is not earning profits.

7. Employees' Compensation provisions of the Code on Social Security, 2020, would apply to some workers as mentioned in the employments listed in the Second Schedule to the Act. So, a watchman protecting the factory or a driver who gets injured during the course of employment and out of acts arising out of employment would be eligible for compensation. Raghuram must plan for these sudden developments and expenses.

8. Payment of Gratuity provisions of the Code on Social Security, 2020, would apply when he has 10 or more employees working for him. He may need to take out an insurance and be prepared to make Gratuity payments upon termination after 5 years, death, or disability of an employee. Fixed Term employees are also eligible for gratuity after termination.

9. Employees' State Insurance provisions of the Code on Social Security, 2020, is now applicable to most establishments having 10 or more employees as given in the First Schedule.

10. Maternity Benefit provisions would apply for shops and establishments having 10 or more employees on any day in the preceding 12 months. He has to ensure that the provisions of the law are followed including payments made upon proof of pregnancy and proof of delivery.

11. Industrial Disputes provisions of the Industrial Relations Code, 2020 would apply. Even an individual worker who is in a supervisory capacity earning an amount not exceeding INR 18,000 p.m. or such amount as notified from time to time can raise an industrial dispute. So too, those engaged in non-managerial and non-administrative roles can raise an industrial dispute. He may have to provide for a grievance redressal system if workers exceed 20 or more. He doesn't have worry about works committee as yet. The number threshold for which is 100 workers.

12. If no manufacturing activity is being carried out then his establishment would not be considered a factory under Factories Act provisions The Occupational Safety, Health and Working Conditions Code, 2020. He must check if the establishment would be covered by the Shops and Establishments Act of the state where he is situated. In which case, he may have to follow the prescriptions as per the State Act regarding timings, leave, and other policies.

13. Trade Unions provisions that are now part of Industrial Relations Code, 2020, would apply to almost all establishments. Raghuram's business would be covered too. However, there is little he can do regarding the unions. He should not interfere or influence the formation of unions, but he would have to eventually work with the employees and their associations by recognizing certain Unions as prescribed. In some cases, he has to recognize a trade union as the sole bargaining agent. When more than one union is present, he may have to constitute a negotiating council.

14. Standing Orders provisions would apply only if the number of employees equals or exceeds 300. However, in some states this has been reduced. So, in Karnataka the number is 50. He must keep track of the number of employees and take action once it exceeds the threshold. Model Standing Orders would be applicable to his firm till his Standing Orders get Certified (after consultations with worker representatives).

15. He should become comfortable with the process of dispute resolution mechanisms. Voluntary arbitration and conciliation are simple and efficient methods for many difficulties.

16. Since his is a small establishment (with less than 50 workers on average in the preceding month) lay-off compensation will not apply but he must be aware of retrenchment compensation and closure procedures that may apply. He should also be aware illegal lock-outs, and other unfair labour practices.

17. Contract Labour provisions would apply only if he has hired contract workers. In the updated Occupational Safety, Health and Working Conditions Code, 2020; 50 or more workers need to be employed as contract workers for applicability of those provisions. It is best for him to ensure basic facilities of drinking water etc. for workers even though his is a new and small firm. Employer is responsible for payment of wages, if the contractor fails to pay. He has to be alert to these aspects.

18. Employees' Provident Funds provisions would apply. The number of employees should equal or exceed 20. If the establishment is a notified estab-

lishment, then too his business would be covered. Those employees drawing above a certain wage would be considered exempted employees.

After examining all the above requirements, Raghuram may just give up. While many issues are certainly complicated, he must recognize that when he is small, there will be fewer laws that apply to his business. As the headcount exceeds 10, more laws would apply. As the number exceeds 20, even more laws would apply. As he grows, he may have help at hand. He can always hire a consultant. The Government is also simplifying the procedures for compliance. A new online portal has been created for small employers. Also, the consolidation of various Acts into four labour codes has substantially simplified matters. In some states, special arrangements are being made to facilitate startups.

Labour Laws (Simplification of Procedure for Furnishing Returns and Maintaining Registers by Certain Establishments) Act, 1988 would certainly be helpful to him till headcount exceeds 40. However, there are several Central Acts that are not covered by this law. For example, Employment Information and Monitoring provisions of Code on Social Security, 2020 possibly would continue to be applicable to his business. Employees' Compensation related provisions and Maternity Benefit and Gratuity related provisions are also possibly relevant.

He can also ensure that he is not employing children below the age of 14 years and no employee or worker is treated as a bonded labor.

There are other Acts too which may apply. Persons with Disabilities are protected and have special rights although this is beyond the enactments with the Ministry of Labour and Employment. There are more aspects to each of the Acts. The above is an illustration of how Raghuram should carry out an analysis of how the labour laws would influence his start up.

ENDNOTES

[i] There is no formal definition of 'Industrial Relations' in primary materials such as the Industrial Disputes Act, 1947 which is now part of Industrial Relations Code, 2020.

[ii] www.aibea.in

[iii] Articles 243G and 243W cover powers given to Panchayats and Municipalities.

[iv] There is no agreed definition of subordinate legislation – loosely it covers the delegated aspects of the Statutes.

[v] Various law commission reports exist in India which attempted to suggest reforms.

[vi] A list of these organizations is available on the Ministry of Heavy Industries & Public Enterprises website.

[vii] Sen, R. (2010, p.201) mentions that PSU workers were reduced since 1991. Please see [4]

[viii] Sen, R. (2010, p.452) too speaks of 'accumulated unemployment'. This happened because 'job growth' was lower than 'workforce growth'.

[ix] Sen, R. (2010, p.541-542) describes how NEP post 1991 created jobs mainly in the unorganized sector.

[x] Ministry of Labour and Employment website – https://labour.gov.in/about-ministry

[xi] A term derived from Adam Smith in his treatise on economics.

[xii] The Ministry of Corporate Affairs and the Ministry of Small and Medium Enterprises provide information on business establishments in India.

[xiii] This was reported in the Times of India of Aug 12, 2017.

[xiv] Central Board of Worker Education Schemes.

[xv] Sen (2010) mentions that SME sector has low unionization.

REFERENCES

[1] Taxmann's, 2018. Labour Laws. Taxmann Publications (P) Ltd.

[2] Annual Report of the Ministry of Labour and Employment. 2017. Labour.nic.in.

[3] Making India a better workplace for all. Electronic Book in PDF form. Ministry of Labour and Employment. Accessed in 2017 from labour.nic.in.

[4] Sen, R. 2010. Industrial Relations – Text and Cases, 2nd Edition, Trinity Press.

ACKNOWLEDGEMENTS

I thank everyone who has inspired and encouraged me in writing the book.

INDUSTRIAL RELATIONS IN MODERN INDIA

This is the first of a series of books on Industrial Relations. India is changing and has a growing economy. People aspects of managing in India is a key challenge for Indian and international companies. How do we do this right? A series of books are planned to encourage readers and professionals to examine and think about effective ways of managing in India.

Industrial Relations In Modern India - New Laws

This book presents the updated labour code in India. New labour codes are being developed and Indian and international professionals are looking forward to great days ahead. Laws are being modified to make it easy to do business.

BOOKS BY THIS AUTHOR

Ideas And Thoughts On Managing

This book describes ideas and thoughts of the author on managing that evolved over several years. It covers ideas related to institutional development, media, mathematics, and industrial relations.

Graphs And Tables For The Modern Manager

Basic mathematical information in the form of tables and graphs is presented in this book.

ABOUT THE AUTHOR

Srikanth Goparaju is a Hyderabad, India based management professional and is interested in subjects such as organizational behavior, change management, and social and economic development.